The one thing you must get right or your business is doomed

How to Use the One-Page Marketing Plan to Boost Repeat Customers, Drive Sales, Revenue and Profit Every Month.

Max McKinzie

Table of Contents

Introduction

In today's world, you no longer have to struggle with long, tedious marketing plans that take months to write and often sit gathering dust. There is a better way: the one-page marketing plan.

When I first heard about one-page marketing plans, I laughed. "How could you possibly fit an entire marketing plan on one page?" But out of curiosity, I tried it. And I have to say, it completely changed my approach to marketing.

I'll never forget the day I finished my very first one-page marketing plan. I sat back in amazement, realizing how much freedom and focus it gave me. All the distractions and unnecessary details were stripped away, leaving only the essentials: my key objectives, the top priorities to achieve them, and the most impactful tactics. I knew exactly what I needed to do to move the needle, and that gave me clarity, confidence, and momentum.

So if you're tired of spending countless hours creating complex marketing plans that you never fully implement, this book is for you. We're going to keep things simple, practical, and actionable. Each section will contain worksheets, templates, and examples to help you create and execute your own one-page marketing plan.

Theodore Roosevelt once said, "In any moment of decision, the best thing you can do is the right thing, the next best thing is the wrong thing, and the worst thing you can do is nothing." Creating a one-page marketing plan will help you do the "right thing," focusing your efforts on what really matters. Don't continue doing nothing and wasting your time on unimportant details. Take action now.

QUOTE

"The real voyage of discovery consists not in seeking new landscapes but in having new eyes." Creating a one-page marketing plan gives you "new eyes" to clearly see what really needs your attention and effort to grow your business.

~ Marcel Proust

Don't worry if you feel overwhelmed at first. My goal is to help fill that one page in small, achievable steps.

We'll start by listing out all your potential marketing objectives and priorities. Then circle the top 3 most important for now. From there, we'll determine the three highest-impact tactics to achieve each objective.

And just like that, you've filled your one page. Once you see how simple and effective this is, you may never go back to those lengthy, unwieldy marketing plans again.

By the end of this book, you'll be ready to fill in your own one-page plan, advance your business to the next level, and reclaim your time, freedom, and focus. It all begins with putting pen to paper—or rather, fingers to keyboard—and getting started.

So what are you waiting for? Grab a notebook, pen, and highlighter, because we're about to journey into the land of simplicity, clarity, and marketing success. One page at a time.

The Tired Old Way vs The One-Page Way

Before we dive into the steps for creating your one-page marketing plan, let's take a look at the pros and cons of the traditional long-form marketing planning approach versus the focused simplicity of the one-page plan.

The Tired Old Way

For decades, marketers have been taught that you need a 100+ page marketing plan filled with details to succeed. You're instructed to gather as much information as possible to complete exhaustive analyses, identify endless objectives, generate never-ending strategies and tactics, and devise KPIs to measure it all.

But does this approach actually work? More often than not, these long, complex plans end up:

➢ Gathering dust on a shelf: You spend months working tirelessly to complete the plan, but then struggle to implement and execute it fully.

➢ Focusing on minutiae, not priorities: You get stuck detailing unimportant tasks while losing sight of what will truly move the needle for your business.

➢ Becoming outdated quickly: All that analysis you did is based on a snapshot in time. By the time you finish the plan, the market will have already shifted.

➢ Causing analysis paralysis: You struggle to determine the "right" objectives, strategies, and tactics amidst endless options and possibilities.

Contrast

Now compare that to the focused simplicity of the one-page marketing plan approach:

It forces you to identify your top 3 priorities: Only the most important objectives and tactics make the cut. You rule out nice-to-haves in order to achieve must-haves.

It's highly actionable. With just 3 objectives and the tactics to achieve them, you actually have a chance of fully executing your plan.

It's nimble and adjustable. Since you constantly evaluate performance, you can tweak your one page regularly based on results and changing conditions.

It cuts through paralysis: By limiting yourself to the essentials that fit on one page, you overcome the overwhelm of unlimited options.

It keeps you focused. By only investing time and effort in your 3 highest-leverage tactics, you avoid spreading yourself too thin.

It provides freedom. With clarity on your top priorities, you have the confidence to say "no" to distractions and lower-impact opportunities.

It accelerates results. By homogenizing on what matters most, you achieve progress much faster than with an unfocused, comprehensive plan.

A traditional 100+ page marketing plan might have seemed like "doing it right" in the past. But in today's fast-paced, unpredictable business environment, a one-page plan is a more effective approach.

Simplicity and focus always trump complexity. The right things, done intensely, achieve far greater results than many things done superficially.

The one-page marketing plan forces you to cut through all the noise and clutter to identify your most high-impact objectives and tactics. And that focus will ultimately lead you to greater clarity, momentum, and business growth.

So throw away your tendency to overcomplicate and overwhelm yourself. Instead, embrace the simplicity, clarity, and nimbleness of the one-page marketing plan. You'll soon see how much more productive, focused, and effective your marketing efforts become.

Common Mistakes to Avoid

Now that you're convinced of the power of the one-page marketing plan approach, you're ready to develop your own.

But before you start filling in that precious single sheet of paper, there are a few common mistakes to steer clear of. Avoiding these pitfalls will help ensure your one-page plan is actually simple, focused, and effective.

Trying to Include Too Much

The biggest mistake people make with one-page marketing plans is trying to include too many objectives, strategies, and tactics. They go against the very spirit of simplicity and end up with a 3-5 page "one-page" plan!

Remember, the power is in the constraints—forcing yourself to only include the 3 most important objectives and the 3-5 most high-impact tactics per objective. Any more than that, and you defeat the purpose.

Objectives Are Too Vague

Occasionally, people state objectives that are vague and immeasurable, like "increase brand awareness" or "generate more leads."

While these may seem like good goals, they're difficult to implement tactics for and impossible to measure success against.

Make sure your objectives are SMART: Specific, Measurable, Attainable, Realistic, and Time-bound.

For example,instead of "generate more leads," aim to "attract 25 new client leads by Q4." Now that you have a clear target, you can align tactics to achieve it.

Tactics Are Too Generic

Similarly, some people include far too many generic tactics that still don't specify enough action.

Instead of simply "running Facebook ads," sharpen your tactics to "run a $500 lookalike audience ad campaign targeting persona X."

The more concrete and targeted your tactics, the easier it will be to implement and optimize them.

Not Regularly Reviewing and Adjusting

Don't set your one-page plan aside and forget it! You must regularly review your objectives and tactics to determine if they're still the highest priorities based on results and changing conditions.

Schedule time on your calendar—perhaps monthly at first—to evaluate your one-page plan. Then adjust what's working, pause what's not, and add any new high-impact tactics you've identified.

Not Translating Into An Action Plan

Your one-page plan is just a framework unless you translate it into a detailed action plan with tasks, owners, deadlines, and resources assigned.

Take the time to spell out the specific steps required to implement each tactic successfully.

For example, for the tactic "run a $500 lookalike audience ad campaign," include tasks like "research personas," "create ad copy," "design ad images," "set budget and schedule," etc. Assign an owner to each task and add deadlines.

Treating it As The "Whole Plan"

Finally, remember that your one-page plan is just that—one page. It contains your highest-level objectives and most impactful tactics.

But you'll likely need to supplement it with other plans for areas like operations, team management, content creation, and more.

Don't make the mistake of thinking your one-page marketing plan is a replacement for all the other plans and systems required to run your business. Rather, it serves as an overarching framework for your top marketing priorities.

So therefore, keep it simple, focused, and concrete. Review and adjust regularly. Translate it into action.

Then supplement with additional plans as needed. When you avoid these common mistakes, your one-page marketing plan has the best chance of accelerating your success.

What's In This Book?

Now that you're excited about creating your own one-page marketing plan, you're probably wondering: What exactly will you learn in this book?

This guide will take you through a step-by-step process to develop your one-page plan.

You'll gain clarity on your most important marketing objectives, generate targeted tactics that will make an immediate impact, and learn how to regularly review and adjust your plan over time.

Section 1: Getting Started

We'll kick things off by providing a sample one-page marketing plan template for you to analyze. This will help you visualize what your final one-page plan might look like.

Section 2: Identifying Objectives

In this section, we'll walk you through a brainstorming and prioritization exercise to surface all your potential marketing objectives.

  Then you'll choose the top 3 most important ones that will make the greatest impact right now.

Section 3: Determining Tactics

For each of your 3 key objectives, we'll generate a list of potential tactics and then circle the 3 most high-impact, "highest leverage" tactics you should focus on. You'll start filling in boxes on your one-page plan!

Section 4: Creating An Action Plan

Here you'll translate each tactic on your one-page plan into a detailed action plan with tasks, deadlines, owners, and resources required. This is what will turn your plan into reality.

Section 5: Executing & Measuring Results

This section provides tips for actually implementing your one-page plan, tracking metrics and KPIs, and evaluating results to determine what's working and what needs adjustment.

Section 6: Reviewing and Adjusting

We'll discuss how and when to regularly review your one-page plan to determine if your initial objectives and tactics are still the highest priorities based on results and changing marketplace dynamics.

Section 7: Expanding & Evolving

As your one-page marketing plan proves effective, this section explores how you can expand it to multiple pages while still maintaining focus, simplicity, and nimbleness. You'll avoid "mission creep" and information overload.

Section 8: Integrating With Operations

Your one-page marketing plan doesn't operate in a vacuum! This section discusses how to integrate it with the operational plans required to actually deliver on your marketing objectives and tactics.

Section 9: Case Studies & Examples

Real-life examples from successful entrepreneurs show you one-page marketing plans in action. You'll gain inspiration and practical templates modeled after plans that worked for growth-hungry businesses just like yours.

Section 10: Next Steps

The book wraps up by providing you with next steps for creating your very first one-page marketing plan from scratch. You'll leave with the knowledge, templates, and motivation to get started immediately.

Overall, this book aims to provide you with the key insights, frameworks, and step-by-step guidance to develop a simple yet powerful one-page plan that actually works for your unique business.

With clarity on the essentials, you'll be poised to gain momentum and make real progress in growing your marketing efforts.

How to Get the Most From This Book

You now have an overview of what you'll learn in this book and how it will guide you in creating your one-page marketing plan. But to really get the most value and impact from the content, here are some specific tips and suggestions:

Start With The End In Mind

Before you dive into the steps and worksheets in this book, take 5–10 minutes to envision your ideal outcome.

Imagine you've already created your one-page marketing plan, and it's working flawlessly. What does it look like?

How has it helped you clarify priorities and accelerate results? Hold that end goal in your mind and revisit it regularly as you work through the book.

Focus On Progress, Not Perfection

Don't get caught up trying to make your one-page plan "perfect" from the start. Your initial plan will likely evolve and improve over time. The most important thing is taking that first step and gaining momentum.

Avoid Overthinking

Don't over-analyze each objective and tactic. Keep it simple, clear, and concrete. You can refine and expand things in future iterations of your plan. For now, just identify the essentials you need to take action on.

Customize For Your Unique Context

While using the templates and examples in this book, adjust the objectives, strategies, and tactics to match your specific business, goals, and audience. Don't try to implement things wholesale that don't truly fit your situation.

Implement Tactics One By One

Don't attempt to execute all the tactics in your one-page plan at once. Choose the single highest-leverage tactic, implement it fully, and then move onto the next one. This allows you to optimize each tactic based on your learning.

Review weekly and adjust monthly.

Set a weekly reminder to review your plan and track results and metrics. Then schedule time on your calendar each month (or quarter) to evaluate if your objectives and tactics still deserve their place on your "sacred one page." Are any changes needed?

Evaluate Based On Effort vs. Impact

When deciding whether to keep or cut tactics from your plan, weigh effort required vs. impact achieved. High-effort, low-impact tactics are the first to go. Low-effort, high-impact tactics should stay.

Get Input From Your Whole Team

Don't create your one-page plan in isolation. Involve your team members, who will implement parts of it. Their feedback and fresh perspectives may surface even higher-impact tactics you hadn't considered.

Treat Your One Page As Sacred Ground

Guard your one page jealously. Avoid letting "nice-to-have" but lower-impact initiatives sneak their way in and distract you from your most important work.

Focus On Progress, Not Perfection

Don't rest on your laurels once you've created your one-page plan. Review and evolve it continuously to keep up with a rapidly changing environment. But focus more on making progress than always pursuing perfection.

That is to say, start with a vision for what success will look and feel like when your plan is working. Then keep it simple, customize it, implement it one tactic at a time, and review or adjust it regularly. Your one-page plan is a framework; the steps you take to fill it in and bring it to life are what really matter.

With these tips in mind, you're now ready to begin developing your own focused, high-impact, one-page marketing plan!

The Secret to Marketing Success

The Not-So-Secret Secret

Throughout this book, I've been encouraging you to strip away unnecessary details, prioritize what matters most, and focus your efforts on just a few high-leverage tactics.

But why does this work?
Why are simplicity and focus so effective?

The simple answer is that focus is the secret to marketing success.

Focus Is The Secret Ingredient

Focus is the X-factor that separates the best marketers from the rest.

It's what takes your efforts from "pretty good" to truly outstanding.

As the old saying goes, "concentration is the mother of all good things." When you intensely focus your energy and resources on your most important priorities, that's when success suddenly accelerates.

An Unfocused Marketing Plan Is Doomed To fail.

Marketing plans that try to be everything to everyone ultimately succeed at nothing. They spread energy too thin and fail to make a meaningful dent.

In contrast, a focused marketing plan hones in like a laser
On the few areas that will make the biggest difference. By homing in on your "main thing", you gain clarity, cut through clutter, and achieve real results.

Focus Forces You To Say "No"

When forced to fit your priorities onto just one page, you must have the discipline to turn away from everything that doesn't belong there. And saying "no" to the right things is arguably more important than saying "yes."

Focus Is Scarce But Powerful

Paradoxically, achieving true focus requires sacrificing other options, and that's not easy in today's world of infinite distractions and possibilities.

But developing the ability to focus your attention, message, and efforts is perhaps the most powerful skill in business today.

Focus Unleashes Your Most Valuable Asset: Your Time And Attention

When you focus on the essentials that fit on one page, you reclaim your mental and practical bandwidth to put your whole self into executing those high-leverage tactics that will make the biggest impact.

And that ultimate focus of your time, energy, and imagination—when applied relentlessly to your most important priorities—is the secret ingredient that turns a good marketing plan into a great one, and a great one into a marketing machine that drives exponentially more success.

So remember: the secret to marketing (and business) success lies not in overcomplicating things but in simplifying.

Not in doing more, but in doing less. Not in trying to be everything to everyone, but in knowing exactly who you serve and what truly matters most.

Focus is power. Focus is clarity.

And focus, my friend, is the not-so-secret secret to marketing success.

Chapter 1

Creating Your One-Page Plan

Objective #1: Identify Your Top Priorities

Now that you're convinced of the power of the one-page marketing plan approach, it's time to develop your very own plan. We'll start by identifying your top 3 marketing objectives—the most important goals you want to achieve to grow your business. These will form the foundation of everything that follows, so it's crucial to get them right.

Brainstorming

To begin, grab a pen and paper and spend 5–10 minutes brainstorming every possible marketing objective for your business. Don't censor anything or worry if some seem unrealistically large or too detailed; just write down every goal that comes to mind.

Some examples of marketing objectives could be:

- Increase website traffic
- Attract more leads
- Boost email list size
- Raise brand awareness
- Grow social media followers
- Expand into new customer segments
- Improve customer retention
- Increase referral business

Prioritizing Your Objectives

Now look over your brainstormed list and start to narrow things down. Circle the 10–15 objectives that initially seem most important. These are likely the ones that would have the biggest impact on your business if they were achieved.

Clustering Similar Objectives

Scan your circled objectives and see if any can be combined or reworded.

For example, you might have separate objectives for "growing Instagram followers" and "increasing Facebook fans", but those could be clustered under one larger objective of "expanding social media audience". Combining related objectives will streamline your list.

Measuring Potential Impact

For each remaining objective on your list, assign a score from 1 to 5 based on two factors:

1.) Effort required: How much time and resource investment would be needed to achieve this objective? (1 = low effort, 5 = high effort)

2.) Potential impact: If achieved, how much would this objective grow your business? (1 = low impact, 5 = high impact)

Add up these two scores to calculate an "impact score" between 2 and 10 for each objective. The higher the score, the more that objective deserves a spot on your one-page.

Rank-order Your Objectives

Looking at the impact scores you assigned, rank your objectives from highest to lowest. Your top 3 highest-scoring objectives are likely the most important to focus on immediately in your one-page plan.

Refining Your Top 3 Objectives

Review your #1, #2, and #3-ranked objectives. Do they meet the SMART criteria (Specific, Measurable, Attainable, etc.)? Can you make them even more concrete, targeted, and impactful?

Here are two examples of refining objectives to make them SMART:

- Vague: Increase web traffic
- SMART: Attract 3000 monthly unique visitors to my website by Q2
- Vague: Boost email subscribers
- SMART: Grow my email list by 50% (to 2500 subscribers) within 6 months

Finalize Your Top 3 Objectives

With your objectives now concrete, targeted, and measurable, you're ready to enter them into the "Objectives" section of your one-page marketing plan template.

For example:

Objective #1

Grow email list by 50% (to 2500 subscribers) within 6 months

Objective #2:

Attract 3000 monthly unique website visitors by Q2

Objective #3

Expand the social media audience by 30% across all channels by year's end.

Moving Forward

You now have the foundation of your one-page marketing plan—your 3 most important marketing objectives that will form the basis of everything that follows.

In the next section, we'll generate specific, high-impact tactics for achieving each objective that you can include on your one page.

But first, take a moment to feel a sense of accomplishment for identifying your most critical priorities. You've taken a huge first step towards creating a marketing plan that will actually work!

Objective #2: Generate High-Impact Tactics

Pick The Right Tactics

Now that you've identified your top 3 marketing objectives for the next 6–12 months, it's time to determine the specific tactics you'll employ to achieve each one.

For each objective on your one-page marketing plan, you'll select 3 tactics, for a total of 9 across your 3 objectives, that are:

- Highest leverage: This will have the biggest impact on achieving the objective

- Easiest to implement: You can take action on them quickly

- Lowest cost: Don't require huge budgets

Generate A Long List of Tactics

For each objective on your plan, brainstorm as many possible tactics as you can think of, regardless of feasibility. You'll narrow things down later.

For the objective "Grow email list by 50% within 6 months", example tactics could be:

- Run Facebook ad campaign targeting "signup" action
- Offer a lead magnet like an ebook to capture emails
- Add email signup form to homepage and landing pages
- Create sequences of useful, educational email nurture campaigns
- Partner with influencers in your industry to acquire subscribers from their lists
- And more!

Cluster and Combine Similar Tactics

Scan your list of tactics for any that can be combined or reworded for simplicity.

For example, you might decide to merge "toolkit giveaway" and "checklist lead magnet" into one larger tactic of "offer a high-value lead magnet".

Evaluate Each Tactic Using 3 Factors

For every tactic on your list, rate it on a scale of 1 to 5 based on 3 factors:

1.) Effort required
2.) Potential impact
3.) Implementation ease

- Add the scores from each factor to calculate a "tactic score" from 3 to 15 for that tactic
- The higher the score, the more that tactic deserves a place on your one-page

Prioritize Tactics By Score

Look at the scores you've assigned and rank your tactics from highest to lowest for that marketing objective.

Your top 3 highest-scoring tactics are likely the "highest leverage" ones for your priority objective.

Circle The winning Tactics

For each marketing objective on your one-page plan, circle the top 3 highest-scoring tactics you'll actually take action on over the next 6–12 months.

Refine Your Chosen Tactics

Take a close look at the 9 tactics you've selected across your 3 objectives. Can you improve any by making them more specific, targeted, or measurable?

For example, refine the tactic:

"Run   social   media   ads"

To:

> "Run $200/month Facebook and Instagram lookalike audience ads targeting personas A and B"

Enter Tactics Onto Your One-Page Plan Template

Now fill in the 3 selected tactics for achieving each objective on your one-page marketing plan template under the "Tactics" column for that objective.

For example:

Objective #1: Grow email list by 50% (to 2500 subscribers) within 6 months

- Offer lead magnet ebook on "Top 10 Marketing Hacks."
- Launch automated email nurture campaign
- Run a Facebook "signup" conversion ad.

These specific, targeted tactics will form the basis of your action plans and execution over the coming months.

Focusing your efforts here instead of spreading them too thin is how you'll make real progress on each objective.

The key is to ruthlessly prioritize tactics that have the greatest chance of moving the needle, require the least effort to implement, and cost the least to put into action.

By selecting your highest leverage, easiest, and cheapest tactics, you're priming your plan for success from the very start!

Objective #3: Fill In Your Sacred One Page

Your "Sacred" One Page

You now have your 3 most important marketing objectives and the top 3 tactics for each—a total of 9 essential priorities that deserve a place on your one-page marketing plan.

It's now time to translate those 9 items into the structured framework of an actual one-page plan you can reference and act upon.

The One-Page Marketing Plan Template

We'll use this simple template with three columns for Objectives, Tactics, and Metrics:

Objectives	Tactics	Metrics
Objective #1	Tactic #1 Tactic #2	Metrics #1 Metrics #2 Metrics #3

	Tactic #3	
Objective #2	Tactic #1 Tactic #2 Tactic #3	Metrics #1 Metrics #2 Metrics #3
Objective #3	Tactic #1 Tactic #2 Tactic #3	Metrics #1 Metrics #2 Metrics #3

Populating The Template With Your Priorities

Using your prioritized list of objectives and tactics, fill in the template:

A. Objectives column: List your top 3 marketing objectives

B. Tactics column: For each objective, enter the 3 highest-leverage tactics you'll employ to achieve it.

C. Metrics column: Determine any key metric you'll measure to evaluate each tactic's effectiveness.

For example:
(Objectives   Tactics   Metrics)

Objectives

Grow email list by 50% (to 2500 subscribers) within 6 months

Tactics

Offer lead magnet ebook
Launch automated email nurture campaign
Run Facebook "signup" ad

Metrics

Subscriber gain
Sequence open/click rates
Unsubscribe rate
Lead volume

Objectives

Expand social media audiences by 30% across all channels by year's end

Tactics
Run lookalike ad campaigns
Post consistent, high-quality content

Metrics
Follower gain
Engagement rate
Share/reply count

I know what you'll be asking: "Why are Tactics grouped under each Objective?" Don't worry, I'll explain.

The tactics are grouped under each objective for a few reasons:

1. Clarity and focus: Having the tactics directly beneath each objective helps keep them aligned and targeted towards achieving that particular goal. It avoids tactics becoming misaligned or scattered between objectives.

2. Accountability: Each objective essentially "owns" the 3 tactics directly underneath it. This makes it clear which tactics are being employed to achieve each specific objective.

3. Measurement: The metrics column next to the tactics helps you determine if each tactic is effective at contributing to the overarching objective it's grouped under.

4. Implementation: Organizing the tactics this way makes it easier to take action on and implement each set of three tactics grouped under an objective.

5. Review and adjustment: When you regularly review your one-page plan, evaluating and potentially changing tactics is easiest when they are clearly grouped under each objective.

So, grouping the tactics directly under each objective provides:

- Clarity and focus
- Alignment and accountability
- A way to measure effectiveness of tactics
- Ease of implementation
- Simplicity during review and adjustment

The grouping helps maintain the hierarchical relationship between your objectives (the "what") and tactics (the "how"). Objectives represent the higher-level goals, while tactics are the specific actions taken to achieve each objective.

You could also translate your one-page marketing plan into an Excel spreadsheet instead of a physical piece of paper. There are a few benefits to this approach:

A. It's editable: You can easily update and adjust your objectives, tactics, and metrics over time as needed.

B. It's sortable: You can sort the data by priority, timeline, owner, metric, etc. to analyze it in different ways.

C. It incorporates formulas: You can add formulas to automatically calculate totals, percentages, growth rates, etc. based on your metrics.

D. It integrates with other tools. You can export the data from Excel and import it into project management, CRM, or marketing automation tools.

A basic Excel setup for your one-page plan could be:

Columns A through C:

A. Objective: List your 3 marketing objectives

B. Tactics: For each objective, list the three tactics you'll employ

C. Owner: Assign an owner for each tactic

In columns D through F:

D. Deadline: Add deadlines or timelines for implementing each tactic

E. Resources: Detail any resources (budget, team members, tools, etc.) required for each tactic

F. Metrics: List the key metrics you'll use to evaluate the success of each tactic

You could then add additional columns for notes, current status, next steps, and more.

The key is to have your objectives in rows, with each corresponding tactic in the row below. This allows you to easily see all the data needed to accomplish a single objective.

Then, by sorting the spreadsheet by column B (Tactics), you can view it organized by tactic instead to get a different perspective.

Overall, an Excel-based approach provides many of the benefits of a one-page marketing plan, but with the advantages of being digital, editable, and integratable with other tools.

Guarding Your One Page

Once you've filled in your template, print it out or make it the background on your computer.

This sacred piece of paper contains the essence of everything that truly matters right now for growing your business.

Guard it jealously, and avoid letting anything unrelated infiltrate your objectives or distract from your tactics.

Revisit and regularly review your one page, but make no changes lightly.

Only update your priorities when results, experience, or the market dictate that something no longer belongs on that sacred ground.

With discipline and focus, your one-page marketing plan can become a powerful catalyst that accelerates you towards your goals.

All that's required now is translating this framework into concrete actions and executing on your highest priorities.

Chapter 2

Bringing Your Plan to Life

You've now identified your top 3 marketing objectives, determined the 3 highest-leverage tactics for each, and filled in your one-page plan template, it's time to bring that plan to life.

Translating Tactics Into An Action Plan

Your one-page marketing plan contains high-level tactics for achieving your objectives, but now you must translate each tactic into a detailed action plan you can actually implement.

This process turns your tactics from good intentions into concrete steps that move you toward your goals.

Step 1: Break Down Tactics

For each tactic on your one-page plan, list out every individual task or step required to successfully execute it. Be as specific and detailed as possible.

For example, break down the tactic "Run Facebook 'signup' ad" into tasks like:

- Research target audience personas and interests
- Create 3-5 ad images and draft ad copy
- Set ad objectives (lead generation, conversions)
- Determine budget ($200/month) and schedule a 2-week initial test period.
- Create ad campaign in Facebook Ads Manager
- Set up Facebook pixel to track website signups

Having a comprehensive list of every microtask helps overcome that initial "where do I even start?" feeling that paralysis and procrastination stem from.

Step 2: Assign Owners

Next to each task you identified, note who is responsible for completing it. This ensures nothing falls through the cracks and keeps team members accountable.

For tasks you'll complete yourself, simply write your own name next to them. But delegate any tasks that others on your team are better suited for.

Separate the different "owning" team members to make the plan even clearer:

You: Draft ad copy and set metrics in Ads Manager.

Designer: Create 3 ad images

Developer: Integrate Facebook pixel

Step 3: Add Deadlines

Alongside each action item owner, note the deadline for completing that task. Putting hard due dates on your calendar keeps you and your team accountable to the timeline required to achieve your one-page objectives.

Step 4: Identify Necessary Resources

Some tasks will require allocating budgets, hiring outside help, or purchasing tools or software. Note any resources needed next to each task. This prepares you for what's required to bring your plan to life.

Using this process to generate a detailed action plan for each tactic on your one-page marketing plan ensures nothing gets lost in translation. You'll have a roadmap of next steps to guide you as you turn tactics into reality and progress toward your goals.

Executing, Measuring and Adjusting

Now that you have clear action plans for each tactic on your one-page marketing plan, it's time to put those plans into action.

This involves three key steps:

1) Implement each tactic sequentially

2) Measure key metrics along the way

3) Adjust tactics based on what's working

Let's dive into each of these in detail:

Implement Tactic By Tactic

Don't try to execute all the tactics on your one-page plan simultaneously. That will spread you too thin and likely result in little progress.

Instead, choose the single highest-leverage tactic based on your "tactic scores" from before. Implement that tactic fully, track your key metric to evaluate results, and then iteratively improve the tactic if needed.

Once you've optimized that initial tactic, move on to executing the next highest-leverage tactic on your plan. And repeat the process.

For example:

1) Implement your #1 tactic for Objective #1. Run that Facebook "signup" ad campaign fully.

2) Move to your #2 tactic for Objective #1. Launch that email nurture campaign.

3) Then execute your #3 tactic for Objective #1: offer that ebook lead magnet.

This sequential approach allows you to:
- Focus your full energy and resources on one tactic at a time
- Learn what works and optimize that tactic before moving on to the next

- Avoid the overwhelm that comes from trying to juggle multiple initiatives simultaneously

Measure Key Metrics Along The Way

As you implement each tactic sequentially, be sure to track your identified key performance metric from your one-page plan. This will indicate whether the tactic is performing well and moving you toward your objectives.

For example, if your metric for the "Facebook ad" tactic is "lead volume", track how many qualifying leads are generated each week from that ad. Are you on track to achieve your email list growth objective?

If not, that's a signal to iteratively improve the ad or consider replacing that tactic with something more effective. But you'll only know by measuring the right metrics as you execute each tactic.

Adjust Tactics Based On Results

Approximately every 4–8 weeks, revisit your one-page marketing plan and evaluate:

1) Are your objectives still the highest priorities?

2) Are your current tactics the most effective ways to achieve each objective?

3) Based on metrics and market changes, should you keep, improve, or replace any current tactics?

Make adjustments as needed. For example:
A. If a tactic isn't performing, iteratively improve it. Tweak the ad copy, increase the budget, narrow the targeting, etc. Then remeasure.

B. If performance still doesn't improve after iterations, replace that underperforming tactic with a new, higher-leverage option from your original brainstormed list.

C. For objectives or tactics that are working well, keep them, but look for ways to double down and turbocharge their impact.

This cycle of executing, measuring, reviewing, and adjusting your one-page marketing plan on a regular basis is what keeps it nimble, focused, and effective over time. The key is establishing that rhythm from the very start and maintaining the discipline to follow it.

Sequential execution, metric tracking, and iterative improvement are the three pillars that turn your one-page plan from ideas on paper into real progress toward your objectives.
  Stay focused on your high-level goals, but be ruthless in analyzing which tactics are truly working and replacing those that aren't, no matter how much initial thought you put into

them. Progress, not perfection, will always drive the greatest results.

Overcoming Resistance and Objections

Even with a clear, one-page marketing plan, actually executing on it can be difficult. Here are some common objections people have and how to overcome them:

"I Don't Have Enough Time!"
Whatever time you do have, whether it's 15 minutes or a few hours each week, prioritize working on your highest-leverage tactics from your one-page plan first.

Calculate how much time you realistically have to devote to your plan each week, then ruthlessly carve that time out of your schedule and guard it jealously. Even small wins in the right places can make a difference over time.

"I'm Not Sure Where To Begin!"
Start with the simplest tactic from your plan—the one with the lowest hanging fruit. Pick just one task from that detailed action plan and accomplish it this week. Any forward progress is better than none at all.

"This All Seems Overwhelming!"

Don't think about executing everything in your plan at once. Implement each tactic one at a time fully before moving onto the next.

Break larger initiatives down into small, achievable steps you can check off your to-do list. Crossing off even one step per day will keep the momentum going.

"I'm Not Seeing Any Results Yet!"

Rome wasn't built in a day. Because you're prioritizing high-leverage tactics, remain optimistic that your initial efforts, even if they don't immediately generate measurable outcomes, are moving you in the right direction.

Stay the course for at least 3–6 months before evaluating if changes to your plan are warranted. For now, just keep executing!

"My Team Isn't On Board"

Explain the Why behind your one-page plan. How will achieving these objectives and tactics help grow the business and benefit your team directly?

Show team members the high-level plan and ask for their input on tactics. Having buy-in from the start increases ownership and follow-through when assigning tasks.

"My Boss Won't Approve it."
Explain the What, how, and Why of your one-page plan:

- What objectives do you want to achieve, and why are they important?
- How the specific tactics you've outlined will help reach those objectives
- Why this focused, high-impact approach is the best use of resources right now

Provide measurements for how you'll track progress and results. The more data-driven you can be, the easier it will be to gain approval.

With persistence and patience, you can overcome any resistance that arises when executing your one-page marketing plan.

Start small, celebrate wins, adjust course when needed, and empower others along the journey. Focus on consistent progress, not overnight success, and bit by bit, you'll achieve meaningful results towards your objectives.

Chapter 3

Evolving Your One-Page Plan

Periodically Reviewing and Adjusting

Your One-Page Plan Is A Living Document. Your initial one-page marketing plan is a great starting point, but it will need continual review and adjustment to stay relevant over time.

Review Your Plan Every 1-3 Months

A. Set a reminder to revisit your one-page plan approximately every 4 to 12 weeks. During this review, evaluate:

- Are your objectives still the highest priorities?
- Are your tactics still the most effective ways to achieve each objective?

- Based on results and changes in the marketplace, should any objectives or tactics be added, improved, or replaced?

Review Your Metrics First

Study the key metrics you identified for each tactic in your plan. What do the numbers indicate?

- Which tactics are performing well and deserve continuation?
- Which tactics are underperforming and likely need improvement or replacement?

Assess External Market Dynamics

Consider whether any changes in your industry, customer needs, or competitive landscape suggest your objectives no longer deserve the highest priority.

Make Adjustments Where Needed

Based on your plan review, execute any of these adjustments:

A. Improvement: Iterate existing tactics that are underperforming but show potential

B. Replacement: Swap out tactics that aren't working for higher-leverage options

C. Evolution: Reevaluate objectives and replace those no longer fitting your greatest needs

D. Expansion: Identify new objectives and tactics that deserve a place on your expanded plan

Record Notes During Your Review

Take notes during each plan review to capture any learnings, ideas for improvement, and data used to make decisions.

Refer to these notes the next time you reevaluate your plan to build on your growing base of expertise and what works best for your business.

Expand Your Plan When Objectives Grow

As new, high-impact objectives and tactics arise that don't comfortably fit on one page, expand your plan accordingly.

- Two pages: When 4-5 key objectives demand focus
- Three pages: For 6–8 must-win objectives that move the needle
- More pages: For extensive plans covering all major business units or functions
- Digital file: Eventually transition to a digital plan you can continually update

The key is to still maintain a "one-page mindset" of simplicity, even as your physical plan grows. Resist "mission creep," where non-essential initiatives find their way into your central plan.

By routinely reviewing and adjusting your one-page marketing plan, you'll keep it dynamic and aligned with your most important priorities over time, ensuring it remains an effective North Star for navigating changing market conditions and driving your business forward.

Expanding Your Plan When Needed

Knowing When To Expand Your One Page
Over Time, new opportunities and priorities may arise that deserve attention beyond what comfortably fits on your original one-page marketing plan.

When this happens, there are two options:

1) Stay at one page but sacrifice some important initiatives
2) Expand your plan to two pages or more to accommodate additional priorities.
     Balancing these two options involves weighing tradeoffs:

a. Staying at One Page

Pros:
- Maintains simplicity and focus
- Forces discipline of saying "no" to less important work

Cons:
- Risks leave impactful opportunities on the table
- May cause frustration that your plan is too limited

b. Expanding Your Plan
Pros:
- Accommodates new, high-impact objectives and tactics
- Avoids blocking growth opportunities

Cons:
- Adds some complexity and potential for mission creep
- Requires extra discipline to keep non-essential items off the plan

When To Make The Move to Two Pages

Some signs you likely need a two-page plan:

A. You have 4-5 truly mission-critical marketing objectives

B. Your review process uncovers numerous high-leverage tactics that don't currently fit on one page

C. Saying "no" to worthwhile opportunities is hampering growth

Structure Of A Two-Page Plan

Page 1:
- Original objectives and highest-priority tactics from one-page plan

Page 2:
- 1-2 additional objectives that have risen in importance
- 3 tactics for each new objective
- Allow some page 2 objectives and tactics to "graduate" to page 1 over

time, replacing those achieving maturity

Beyond Two Pages to Three and More

For larger businesses with >5 truly must-win marketing objectives:

- Transition to a 3+ page plan to accommodate all essential priorities
- Consider a digital file that allows for easy expansion and updating versus physical prints

Know when expansion of your plan is a liberation versus a distraction. Proceed cautiously, but pull the trigger when new opportunities truly demand it.

And maintain the "one-page mindset" of simplicity and focus, only now spread across multiple,organized pages. This keeps your expanded plan from spiraling into "everything and the kitchen sink."

Integrating With Operations

Aligning your plan With business operations For your one-page marketing plan to truly succeed, it needs buy-in and integration with the operations side of your business.

Marketing alone can't achieve objectives; they require executing on tactics that span departments like product, sales, customer success, and beyond.

The Divide Between Marketing And Operations

Unfortunately, marketing and operations often operate in silos with misaligned goals. This leads to:

A. Ambiguous accountabilities
B. Duplicated or conflicting work
C. Lack of cross-functional collaboration
D. Missed opportunities due to lack of coordination

Bridging The Gap With A Unified Strategy

To overcome these issues, connect your one-page marketing plan to the strategy of your overall business in three ways:

1) Align objectives. Ensure that marketing objectives support broader organizational goals.
2) Share plan. Socialize your one-page plan with operations leaders to gain buy-in and input.
3) Collaborate on tactics. Involve operations in determining tactics that require cross-team execution.

Aligning Objectives

Begin by mapping your marketing objectives (grow leads, boost referral volume, increase retention, etc.) to how they:

A. Support revenue goals
B. Impact key performance metrics
C. Enable product or service objectives
D. Demonstrate value for customers

Once objectives are aligned, socialize your one-page plan with:

- CEO/Leadership team
- Sales, customer success and product/R&D leads

Explain how achieving your objectives will help them achieve theirs. Work together to refine objectives as needed to align goals.

Collaborating On Cross-Functional Tactics

Discuss tactics with operations that:

- Require sales/success team participation
- Implicate product or service changes
- Need budgets, resources or approvals from other teams?

Together, determine:

- Task owners across functions
- Dependencies between teams
- Key metrics to track progress

Make any needed changes directly on your one-page plan to reflect cross-team tactics. Regularly check-in with operations leads to ensure execution is on track.

By aligning objectives, socializing your plan, and collaborating on tactics that span functions, you can gain organizational alignment around your one-page marketing plan.

This unity of purpose will guide integrated execution that ultimately accelerates progress toward goals that benefit the entire business.

Chapter 4

Inspiration and Examples

Beyond reviewing your own metrics and making adjustments based on results, it can also be helpful to gain inspiration from how others have successfully implemented one-page marketing plans.

Hearing case studies and examples of one-page plans in action can provide:

1. Practical lessons for creating your own customized plan

2. Ways to avoid potential pitfalls

3. Motivation and proof that the approach works

Here are a few types of examples you can draw from:

Case Studies

Reading firsthand accounts of how companies and organizations have used the one-page approach can be illuminating. Ideally, look for case studies that include:

A. The business's original pain point or challenge

B. Their one-page plan's objectives and key tactics

C. Any hurdles they overcame during implementation

D. The clear results they achieved aligned with their objectives

E. Lessons learned: someone creating their own plan could benefit from

Sample One-Page Plans

Coming across actual one-page marketing plans, preferably with some explanation of the business's goals and strategy, can serve as valuable templates.

Study the structure, layout, and level of detail in sample plans to inform how you wish to organize and present yours. But remember, every plan should be customized to your specific objectives and context.

Industry Examples

Finding one-page plans or case studies from businesses similar to your own can be particularly insightful. You'll likely face comparable challenges and opportunities pursuing related objectives.

Seeing how companies in your industry have organized their plans, decided on objectives, and selected high-impact tactics can motivate and guide your own efforts.

Personalized Coaching

For the most tailored inspiration, consider working directly with a one-page marketing plan coach or consultant.

They can help you:

- Identify your most important objectives
- Generate and select the highest-leverage tactics
- Ensure your plan supports your overall business strategy
- Implement and adjust your plan over time for the best results

While examples, case studies, and templates all have value, nothing can replace the customized, expert guidance a dedicated coach can offer in creating a plan tailored uniquely to you.

So seek inspiration from many sources, but remember that your one-page marketing plan will ultimately need to reflect your specific goals, resources, and context to be effective.
  Examples only inform, while trial and error, data, and ongoing review ultimately refine your approach.

Case Studies of One-Page Plans in Action

Real-world examples of one-page plans in action. Hearing how others have successfully used the one-page marketing plan approach can provide inspiration and practical lessons for creating your own.

Here are two case studies:

GrowRevenue Marketing Agency

Pain point: The marketing agency had a bloated strategic plan with over 40 objectives and 100 tactics that was impossible to execute on.

Solution: They created a one-page marketing plan with just 3 key objectives:
1) Grow client base by 15%
2) Expand service offerings to 3 new areas
3) Improve team productivity by 10%

Tactics for each include:
- Launch hub page and campaign for new service
- Run referral incentive program for existing clients
- Implement project management system

Results:
- Focused marketing efforts on their best options

- Streamlined operations around most crucial priorities
- Achieved all 3 objectives within 8 months

Borg Tech Consulting

Pain point: The consulting startup had good ideas but no system for prioritizing and executing them.

Solution: They created a one-page plan with objectives to:

1) Acquire 5 new enterprise clients

2) Build brand awareness among target prospects

3) Double task completion productivity

Tactics include:
- Create targeted LinkedIn ads for new clients
- Launch a sponsored podcast for their industry
- Implement a project management system for task tracking

Results:
- Actionable tactics drove real progress
- Hit all objectives within 12 months
- Productivity gains allowed them to take on more clients while maintain quality

These examples highlight how the one-page approach can:

1. Provide much-needed simplicity and focus

2. Create alignment across teams

3. Accelerate progress by prioritizing the highest-leverage tactics

4. Improve productivity by minimizing wasted time and resources

5. Drive meaningful results towards critical objectives

While every business is unique, these principles remain the same. So use real-world case studies, in addition to your own experimentation, to refine your one-page plan into an engine of growth for your organization.

Sample One-Page Marketing Plan Templates

Using Templates To Kickstart Your One-Page Plan

Exploring sample one-page marketing plan templates can provide structure and inspiration for creating your own.

Review Several Different Template Styles

There are a few common templates you'll find:

Basic Outline Template

Objectives	Tactics
Objective #1	Tactic #1 Tactic #2 Tactic #3
Objective #2	Tactic #1 Tactic #2 Tactic #3
Objective #3	Tactic #1 Tactic #2 Tactic #3

Columnar Template

Objectives	Tactics	Metrics
Objective #1	Tactic #1	Metric #1
	Tactic #2	Metric #2
	Tactic #3	Metric #3
Objective #2	Tactic #1	Metric #1
	Tactic #2	Metric #2
	Tactic #3	Metric #3
Objective #3	Tactic #1	Metric #1
	Tactic #2	Metric #2
	Tactic #3	Metric #3

In this version, the three main sections (Objectives, Tactics, and Metrics) are clearly labeled and organized in a table format. Each objective is listed in the first column, followed by the corresponding tactics in the second column, and the metrics used to measure success in the third column.

Note that the template can be customized based on the specific goals and metrics of your business.

This template structures a one-page marketing plan into 3 key parts:

1) Objectives: The main goals you want to achieve

These are your top 3-5 marketing priorities, for example, "Grow our email list by 20%" or "Increase customer retention by 10%".

2) Tactics: The specific actions you will take to meet each objective

For each objective, you list the 3 tactics that will help you achieve that goal.

Tactics are things like "Launch an email nurture campaign" or "Run Facebook ads".

3) Metrics: How will you measure the success of each tactic?

For each tactic, you identify a key metric that shows if that tactic is working or needs improvement.

Metrics could be things like "Email list growth per month" or "Customer churn rate".

So put together, it would look something like this:

Objective:
Grow our email list by 20%
Tactics:
Launch email nurture campaign
Offer lead magnet ebook
Run Facebook "signup" ad

Metrics:
    Email list growth per month
    Lead form submission rate
    Ad conversion rate

By structuring your plan this way - linking each objective to its tactics and metrics - you can easily evaluate what's working, what needs improvement, and make adjustments to achieve your objectives.

Prioritize What Fits Your Needs

Review multiple templates and pick the one that:

- Is easiest for you and your team to update
- Aligns best with how you think about your objectives and tactics
- Provides the right level of structure without being overly constraining

Then customize that template to fit your specific context. For example, you could:

- Add columns for timelines, budgets or task owners
- Include quarterly milestones for objectives
- Number tactics within objectives for easier reference

Bring The Template To Life With Your Priorities

Once you've chosen and customized a template, populate it with:

- Your 3-5 most important marketing objectives
- The 3 highest-leverage tactics for achieving each objective
- Key metrics for evaluating each tactic's success

Your completed template becomes your actionable one-page marketing plan—a focused roadmap to guide you towards your top priorities and measure progress.

Sample one-page plan templates provide a useful starting point: structure, columns, and examples to inspire your own.

But always remember to customize the level of detail, category titles, and overall presentation to best support your goals, team, and context.

What truly matters are the objectives, tactics, and metrics you populate that template with, not the template itself.

Chapter 5

Key Secrets to Consistently Getting Tons of FREE Exposure

Contrary to popular belief, it is really rather simple to get regular media attention. The game has rules, just like anything else. The majority of the regulations are confidential, which is the only issue. They take years to find on your own and are not documented.

KEY SECRET #1

You need to write genuine news articles regarding your goods or services.

Remember that providing news to their viewers is the main duty of radio, television, newspapers, and magazines. While certain media outlets may also provide entertainment, their main goal is to provide their specific audience with news that is valuable. This implies that you need to transform the message about your good or service into information that would be interesting to the media. Be at ease: this does not imply that you will need to employ a television anchor or reporter to assist you in producing news. All you need to do is come up with a news perspective to showcase your knowledge.

There is now one more component required to succeed at this point. The audience of your chosen medium must find your news to be really interesting. Products often provide a wide range of enticing features or advantages. If you focus your news on what will most benefit the readers of your medium, you will have a higher chance of gaining attention.

The greatest strategies for creating news are to create a story aspect around your product or service that will either:

A. Address a critical issue that the viewer is experiencing.
B. Teach the audience how to accomplish a really desired objective.
C. Give something to the audience.

A bit more explanation is required for the third point. Offering anything for free is an effective PR tool. Individuals like receiving free items. Offering free samples, free demos, free instructional pamphlets, and free consultations are all very effective ways to elicit a response from your prospects.

Using a free offer also greatly boosts your chances of being covered by the media, which is another clear benefit. Giving anything out to their viewers is something that editors and station managers like doing, particularly when it comes at your cost.

Thus, give this potent weapon a try if you wish to gain more coverage. Developing a news perspective that combines all three of these components is essential if you want to go all out and get the greatest amount of coverage.

KEY SECRET #2

You Need to Develop and Execute a Robust PR Strategy

Alright, so Key Secret #1 was really rather simple—a piece of cake. However, when Key Secret #2 is revealed, things go nasty. I can only imagine the curses you are bringing up against my ancestry. In the end, nobody likes planning, and even fewer of us really undertake any planning at all.

Please give me a moment. I'll walk you through creating your PR strategy in a reasonably straightforward manner in a moment. More significantly, however, I want to demonstrate to you why it's imperative that you set aside time in advance to draft a PR strategy.

Here's why:

The effectiveness with which you organize and execute your campaign will directly correlate with the amount of worthwhile media attention that you are able to secure!

You will not be able to choose the kind of publicity you get if you do not have a strategy. It will either be serendipity or the capricious judgment of a media decision-maker that determines the publicity you get. Establishing a sound, uncomplicated plan gives you some influence over where you get coverage. You can behave positively when you have a strategy. No strategy minimizes your efforts to respond to feeble responses from external factors.

It is easy to create a PR strategy. A little homework is all that is required.

Choose the target or audiences that will be most likely to purchase your product or service.

Choose every piece of media that each audience reads, watches, and listens to. (I'll provide you with the exact instructions to do this in Key Secret #3.)

Establish a fair timetable for getting in touch with each of these media outlets. This ought to span three to six months.

Observe your timetable and monitor your progress. You may find a form to plan out your timetable and monitor your progress in Sample Number 2, which is attached to this report.

Follow up with the media outlets that have the potential to consistently bring you the most money.

You'll question why you put off creating a PR strategy for so long until you realize how easy it is. As you can see, it's rather simple to do. Which brings me to the point: don't be fooled by its simplicity. Even a basic scheme like the one in the example might have powerful effects.

This is the reason why:

It first compels you to plan out your whole schedule for the following three to six months in a clear and rational manner. Making a route chart ensures that you are aware of your starting point and your destination.

Secondly, it simplifies the task of maintaining an efficient, continuous campaign. All you have to do is arrange for your responsibilities to be completed on time.

Thirdly, it provides you with a plethora of outstanding feedback and is an amazing management tool.

For example, "Which media consistently react to your promotions?"

"How long does it take for major media outlets to react?"

Which media outlets provide such impressive outcomes that you should prioritize them more highly?

KEY SECRET #3

How to Utilize Your Media Sources to Their Fullest Potential

If you've read any other books or studies on obtaining exposure, you'll notice that most of them advise you to establish business connections with as many media outlets as you can. and to provide a call after each press release. I think that's a bunch of bullshit.

First of all, if you think along such lines, you won't have time for anything else in your firm but to manage your PR campaign! It really simply comes down to time management and common sense when it comes to making the most of a successful PR campaign.

This is the actual method for completing tasks. A combination shotgun/rifle strategy is required.

Using the shotgun method first:

You'll need to compile a list of all the magazines, newspapers, radio shows, and television shows you would want to include in order to execute this part of your campaign. You should submit copies of every press release you create to these outlets.

Use the following websites and reference materials to do this:

1. News, Services, and Information from Bacon's Media
2. The Publicity of Bacon Checking
3. GEBBIE PRESS HUDSON'S NEW SCHOLARLY
4. U.S. Publicity Directory Standard Periodical Directory Working Press of the Nation

After compiling your list, you should choose 10 contacts that are significant enough that you may wish to give them a call. This is your list of targets to shoot in the eyes. When this list is used properly, it may help with successful time management.

You'll be using overworked, stressed-out media sources who are under pressure to meet unreasonable deadlines. It often takes ten or twenty phone calls to reach one of these sources.

Indeed, you can generally expect this! As you can see, this procedure might take a long time. Therefore, in order to prevent this from turning into an excessive undertaking, you need to use extreme caution when choosing the sources for your follow-up calls.

Good news is desperately needed by the media. Every day, they have an enormous amount of area to occupy. Whether or not you contact someone, your chances of receiving coverage for a really acceptable item are quite high since this is always true.

I suggest running a campaign in which you make 95% of your connections just by mail. Use a reply postcard, such as the one in Sample Number 3 at the back of this report, to keep track of your findings. You'll need to decide when it's really worthwhile to spend your precious time attempting to break through the telephone barrier for the remaining 5%.

The following are the factors you should use to decide:

How important is this coverage to you?

What is your chance of winning this coverage?

Small companies and investors would be your usual clients if you sold accounting software for PCs. You wouldn't likely be Johnny Carson's special guest. However, a prominent mention in Business Week, Entrepreneur, or Success may bring in a sizable profit. You should focus on calling those media outlets once you follow up with them.

KEY SECRET #4

This is the primary cause of businesses' inability to get all the necessary free exposure.

Clients ask me, "How do I improve the results of my publicity campaign?" time and time again. The answer is persistence for the great majority of my customers, which probably includes you as well.

See, most individuals want to deceive themselves, even if they already know this. They want to think that I can give them access to some magical knowledge that will make all of their troubles disappear. However, you notice that each time I wave my marketing wand, I always get the same response: persistence.

To be persistent, you must create and adhere to a strong PR strategy. This is the essential component that will provide you with much-needed success. Because it's important to understand that a successful campaign might take up to six months to provide results, often even longer.

Additionally, a PR campaign that is executed in stages is often the most effective. Once again, perseverance is a crucial component. Let's imagine that publishing in widely read national periodicals is your ultimate objective. Send your media kit to each of the important outlets on your list during the first phase.

These will include national, state, and local sources.

While some of these sources won't cover you at all, others will. That is anticipated. Most of the publicity you get in the initial phase will come from regional media outlets. Additionally, you could be exposed to some state-wide and sometimes even national media. However, let's presume that the coverage you get is local for all intents and purposes.

As a shrewd marketer, the next step is to create a clipsheet using quotations from the press coverage you secured in the first round. You now send your media bundle once again, including your clipsheet this time.

You'll discover that things happen with a snowball effect. More publicity results from publicity.

Your credibility is boosted by publicity clips. Additionally, they make your primary sources consider if other sources are providing important information that they aren't. It leads to further press for you as more of these outlets join the bandwagon.

Here's another example of why perseverance is so important. Every week, hundreds of media packets are sent to various media outlets. These people operate quickly and with plenty of material.

They will often hardly notice your first media package, yet your brand or goods may stick in their subconscious. Persistence will eventually lead to the coverage you want, even if it takes two, three, or 10 attempts.

Ingenious Ideas You Can Use to Start Cashing in on Free Publicity Today

1. Give renowned public figures samples of your goods as a donation. Make it

known if you get a response, which is probably from senators and members of Congress.

The media loves stories about well-known individuals.

2. Promote a competition. Restaurants may sometimes award the winner of a worst-recipe contest with supper for four.
3. A weekend excursion might be sponsored by travel companies. Additionally, it's not hard for your company to think up original contest ideas for use as PR.
4. Encourage an award. Publishers of books and other services will find this extremely helpful. However, almost any organization should be able to benefit from this strategy since it can be used for both serious and lighthearted purposes.

5. Appeal to your regional press. Local producers and editors like success tales from home.

Chapter 6

Evaluating Competition

Competitors must be found in order to launch or manage a firm. Rivals have the power to either destroy or build your company. A competition study is an essential component of a business strategy that helps you understand how effectively your company can strategically expand in the market.

Procedures for Assessing Competition

Step 1: Research your local and national rivals in business, particularly in the industry you were thinking about entering. You may find further information about them on websites, trade organizations, business journals, etc.

Step 2: After learning more about the competitors, make an effort to learn more about them, their services, products, and methods for achieving their goals. Find out more about their organizations, businesses, and other endeavors. If at all feasible, study their annual reports since they are essential to understanding their long-term strategy. Recognize their target market, company histories, offerings, financial support and stability, and any other pertinent news.

Step 3: Pay attention to your company's indirect rivals. While indirect rivals are companies that are kind of in the same "field" as you are, direct competitors are companies that are exactly like yours. You want to own and operate a pet store. Pet stores are direct rivals, whereas grooming services, animal hospitals, and clinics are indirect competitors. Pet services are your indirect rivals in this scenario; they won't fight with you for clients, but because the majority of them are located close to your place of business, you can be certain that pet care is in high demand there.

Step 4: Add this report to your company strategy after assessing the competitors and business competition. The competition analysis portion of a business plan might be defensive for your company while offensive to rival companies. If the business plan is intended for investors, you should demonstrate in your research of the competition what you can add or change to entice investors to invest in your company rather than that of your rivals.

Chapter 7

How to price just right–Pricing Strategy

The most crucial choice you will make when attempting to sell anything online is how much to charge for your goods or services. You must compete with the multitude of options that clients have access to via the Internet. Your ability to remain in the market will depend on the pricing you set.

You must have a precise understanding of price. How far are you able to push it? How often should you check the prices? Much would depend on how you manage this business phase.

To start, you need to choose a target market and then project the price range that this group of people is likely to be prepared to pay for your goods or services.

In addition, however, you also need to make sure that you turn a profit for yourself. Additionally, there is a good chance that these two requests will clash. Different individuals determine the cost of their things using different methods. While some of these are supported by science, others do not. One such process, which takes into account consumer expectations, manufacturing costs, and other industry participants, is described below.

The sum of all the costs you incur in producing something is its cost. Costs for raw materials, equipment, packing, shipping, etc. are included in expenses. The price is what clients must pay for each unit of your item or service.

The price has to be higher than the cost in order for you to profit. If you want to operate your business for a long period of time, you should always charge more than it costs, unless there are exceptional circumstances. There are situations when lowering pricing is necessary, such as when entering a market. Offering introductory prices that are less expensive than those of your rivals will draw attention. And you may progressively raise costs if you have a respectable number of clients!

Customers' willingness to pay for your services is closely correlated with how important and valuable they perceive your offering to be. Naturally, a big part of this will be determined by your marketing tactics and reputation in the industry.

Your optimum pricing is somewhere between these two figures—your cost and the amount of money your clients are ready to spend on your goods. In the long term, it would be beneficial for you if your pricing was somewhat less than what your clients were willing to pay for your services.

Since the worth of money is so evident in today's environment, consumers who are shopping for necessities have become conscious of the cash component while making purchases.

They want to receive the most for the least amount of money, so setting your prices appropriately can help you maintain a steady stream of clients and revenue. However, this does not imply that the only way to win over consumers is to lower costs, since this often results in losses.

But more than anything else, a product's value—as perceived by the buyer—determines its price. When looking to purchase a Toyota on the market, someone will expect to receive the greatest bargain from you—they will never expect a high-profile car like a Mercedes to be priced similarly to a Toyota.

Therefore, enhancing any product's value via effective marketing, research, and development is a certain method to guarantee that your customers will recognize and accept the product's value and price. Consequently, all that has to be done is alter the way a buyer perceives a thing.

Giving a price-conscious customer a clear image of the long-term advantages of their purchase is the easiest and most effective way to win them over. Everyone enjoys knowing that they made a wise investment in something that will endure and provide greater rewards. Therefore, if you can persuade the customer that investing in something valuable and long-term is what makes purchasing anything desirable, they will undoubtedly agree to spend the money.

You may just be able to seal the sale by demonstrating how the more expensive item would ultimately cause fewer issues and save a ton of effort and needless money on service and repairs. Once again, the goal is to persuade their clients that by considering the purchase's long-term advantages, they are making the right decision.

Any reasonable consumer will come to you if you have a good product and sell it well. Customers want the finest available for themselves, even if it means shelling out a little more money. Hence, providing high-quality items consistently results in returning consumers.

Recognizing that price is not the only factor in a buyer's decision to purchase is necessary to win over price-sensitive customers. You can showcase the whole worth of your service or client when you take the time to understand their wants. If you don't get the whole picture, you might end up having to address pricing issues, which won't be good for the long-term success of your company.

Know your clientele, then. Discover their desires and how their brains function. This will greatly aid in persuading and courting them to purchase the appropriate, yet pricey, item. If you don't realize that purchasing decisions are influenced by a variety of factors outside of money, as previously indicated, you may need to continually lower costs in order to attract clients, which will not be very beneficial for your company.

How to Achieve "Winning Price"

Choosing a price for your goods or services might be the most important business choice, particularly if you're attempting to sell online. It's not as easy as it sounds to set a price. In order to turn a profit, your pricing must be higher than your costs but less than what your consumers are willing to pay for your service, or what the "market can bear." These considerations must be examined while setting your product's price.

There are complex price schedules that you must comprehend and be able to adhere to.

Your company strategy will determine the price plan you should choose.

such as the "Pricing to Penetrate" strategy. This strategy would be effective for you if your goal is to swiftly enter the target market. You must set a cheap price for your goods in order to accomplish this goal.

Determining how low you can go without reaching the bottom is crucial, however. You must determine the lowest point you may go without incurring significant debt or losses. If you are going to get long-term clients in exchange for your first losses, you shouldn't be concerned about it.

However, how can the lifetime worth of each client be ascertained?

Keep your loyal consumers coming back, and make sure you take action to keep them loyal to your company. In order to leave a lasting impression, penetration pricing is helpful.

When a lot of new competitors are entering the market, it may also be helpful.

Your offering needs to be the best "sticky product" that the consumer can part with. For example, those who get addicted to online brokers don't even consider their other options since they are so much more handy.

Making a product of the highest quality is another way to guarantee that the buyer will come back. For instance, if you were selling books online, you would become well-known right away if your book was excellent and priced well.

For instance, due of their highly subsidized prices, Amazon.com is the dominant participant in the online book shop market. Despite the potential financial costs associated with this business strategy, they have successfully built a reliable clientele that they can now rely on.

Another plausible real-world example is how razor manufacturing businesses realized that selling razor blades instead of handles would be much more lucrative. The rest, as they say, is history.

Pricing According to the Type of Product

The secret to success is determining the appropriate pricing for your goods, both in the short and long terms. The ideal pricing for your goods would fall between what they cost and what a client is willing to pay for them. The price would include the cost of the raw materials as well as additional fixed and variable production charges.

In fact, it may increase your revenues by two or three times the current amount.

Technically, your goods will fit into one of two categories:

Commision

In this industry, there is a lot of rivalry since all of the participants' goods are identical; the only thing that separates them is pricing. You have to be razor-sharp and aware at all times. The only thing that would set you apart is how skilled and effective you are. Something sloppy will cause problems once again.

Proprietary goods

These are real, genuine things that are unique in and of themselves. You compete with other market participants based on the unique advantages of your offerings. You may establish pricing that will guarantee you make the most money if you are competent and in demand.

The online economy is evolving quickly. Due to new competitors, shifting demand, etc., you may need to regularly adjust your rates in order to remain competitive.

Then there are certain things that are both proprietary and commodity, such as computer hardware. Computer systems are becoming more complex and updated on a regular basis, and competition is fierce. It's a proprietary product in that, because of the extra functionality it provides, a Macintosh can nevertheless afford to be much more costly than a typical Windows machine.

In any case, you cannot afford to price your product incorrectly since it might result in its immediate demise on the market.

These days, price battles are an inevitable element of doing business for any corporation. You must always be alert and follow through on your commitments if you want to survive. Everyone must cut their prices if even one rival does so. But you should have good reason to defend yourself if you're not going to. One excellent argument may be a loyal consumer base that would support you no matter what.

Pricing Strategies That Improve Profit

One aspect of the marketing mix that is commonly disregarded is the pricing strategy. They should be taken into account in the same way as marketing and advertising techniques, since they may significantly affect earnings. Changes in pricing have the potential to significantly alter sales volume and gross margins. This has an indirect impact on other costs by, for instance, lowering storage costs or opening up chances for suppliers to provide bulk discounts.

Your best price plan is also determined by other criteria. Think about the five factors—your suppliers, consumers, rivals, and the availability of replacement products—that affect other company choices. It's also important to think about how you want your target audience to view you. If you overcharge for a high-end product, for instance, buyers won't think the quality is sufficient. On the other hand, if value lines are overpriced, consumers will buy the less expensive products offered by other companies.

Several pricing tactics to take into account are:

1. competitive costs

The best way to conduct business is to keep your pricing competitive with that of your rivals. Keep a watch on the prices your neighboring competitors are charging for their goods, and then set your own at a price that is either the same or lower.

2. Price + markup

This strategy, which is the exact opposite of the previous one, tries to set your pricing based on your preferences and the gain percentage you want to retain rather than the market. However, in addition to the benefit of making you a lot of money by establishing low pricing, this might also backfire in some situations. So before you select the price, consider your options carefully.

3. Leader in Loss

Selling comparatively inexpensive goods to consumers who have the opportunity to purchase more at a reduced price is another successful tactic to attract customers and significantly increase sales. How Much to Charge for Your Good or Service Just right pricey items. However, this is a rather short-term agreement that often ends up being a risk.

4. Finish off

When you are cleaning out your inventory, this is an intriguing strategy to give a try. This strategy involves selling your excess inventory at very low prices in order to offset losses.

5. Discounts for trade or membership

Recognize your clients. Make a short list of the people who can bring you profit and provide unique incentives to them in the hopes that they will be persuaded to make further purchases from you and return. Reduce costs, provide discounts, and take other necessary steps to get customers back into your store.

6. Discounts for bulk and bundling.

The basic one plus one free is also quite effective. Thus, provide a sizable discount to a chosen group of clients on bulk purchases of comparable or related things or of the same type, like five shirts. Additionally, to prevent losses, make offers on outdated inventory or combine new and old items to get rid of extras.

7. Iteration

A smart strategy to not just get rid of those models from regular people is to offer several versions of the same fundamental product and then offer reduced pricing for the more basic models. However, in order to serve as an incentive for the high-buying clients, one may also combine offers like free service for a certain amount of time with the more expensive ones.

Price Skimming As a Pricing Strategy

The price plan is one of the most crucial marketing tactics you will use for your company. The appropriate pricing strategy will determine your revenues and market share, in addition to selecting the best product, clever marketing, and a solid sales plan. Market skimming is often used by the top players in a field to determine prices.

A computer manufacturer's plan is to release a new laptop about every eight months. He maintains the price of the new laptops at their introduction higher while lowering the price of the older, unsold models, which are in their mature period. Because the new computers have more functionality, their price will go up.

As a result, the manufacturer is skimming the market and the price at various periods, including introduction, growth, maturity, and decline. By charging the greatest price that each of these phases can get, he makes the most money.

This tactic will be effective in a sizable market with a significant number of consumers, a strong demand for the product or service, and a low-cost organization. In the laptop example above, there is a large market of repeat customers and a cheap cost structure in a technologically advanced business.

The firm is now facing a struggle due to the large number of rivals in this industry. It will be very difficult for customers to evaluate a product's quality, service, and value for money if all of these rivals have an extensive lineup of comparable items, each with a different life cycle.

When presented with an array of identical items, the consumer will choose the laptop that offers the most features at the most affordable cost. Additionally, if your business does not have the lowest price, it might damage the image of your brand by giving the impression that you have been overpricing your items, which will ultimately result in a decline in sales.

Prior to selecting a pricing plan, make sure you thoroughly research the market. It is important to possess a clear understanding of client behavior and the potential actions or reactions of rivals. Additionally, when this strategy is being implemented, it should be checked often to make sure that the underlying assumptions that guided its development have not altered in response to changing market circumstances.

Is the use of psychological pricing a successful strategy?

There is a psychological component to price. Customers tend to think that a thing has more value if it is more expensive. This idea renders pricing tangibles more effective than the actual goods, despite the fact that it is more psychologically based than realistic.

It is noteworthy to note, nevertheless, that as a customer does a more in-depth study of the product's nature, his judgments become more logical, and price no longer serves as a yardstick for evaluating a product's value. Customers often gravitate toward prices that end in uneven values, like $9 or $99, thinking they are receiving a better deal than if the prices ended in even amounts, like $20, $66, etc. This is an excellent illustration of psychological pricing in action.

Product valuation: Products will be deemed more valuable than a $200,00 listing if they are priced in an odd range, such as $199,00, or in a pricing "band," such as those seen in online auctions. The psychology behind these kinds of customer actions is that odd-range pricing is often seen as better value. As a result, you need to be certain that you have selected the appropriate pricing and marketing plan for the product.

Reference pricing is an additional example of psychological pricing. Reference pricing is the process by which consumers connect to a price on a psychological level because it expresses their perception of the link between a product and its price. When it comes to expensive goods, like luxury goods, reference pricing has a significant impact and may be used to the advantage of a whole company.

It is important to use caution when setting pricing, however, since it might backfire if the customer believes the product isn't worthy of that classification. In cases where the product's attributes appeal to buyers who are sensitive to price, reference pricing might be a suitable approach.

High-end luxury goods that appeal to ego-sensitive consumers are one example of this. Making sure that the price you have set for a product suits it best from all perspectives—including your own—is essential for reference pricing to be effective.

Make sure the pricing chosen is appropriate for the product and that it has undergone testing prior to being introduced into the intended market. The impact of different market factors on the cost must also be taken into account. The product has to be appropriate for a psychological pricing strategy; the advertising plan needs to be sufficient for the pricing strategy; and the channels of distribution need to match the price and not be more expensive than the product itself.

Pricing for Market Penetration

Market penetration pricing is a quick-entry pricing approach based on the idea that higher sales volume results from lower prices, which in turn lowers total expenses. This is a practical tactic that works well in marketplaces where prices are sensitive. Take the DVD player industry, for instance. Sales volumes are large, but there are also a lot of rivals in this sector.

The cost of producing DVD players has significantly decreased, and the quick addition of new features and advantages to new models has been made possible by continually advancing technology. All companies that profit from DVD players and offer large quantities of goods at affordable or fair rates are pursuing a market penetration strategy.

By using market penetration pricing, business owners often want to expand both their brand's market share and the market for their product overall. The underlying premise of all computations is that the company with the lowest pricing will have the most market share. However, before using this pricing approach, it is crucial to assess your market, price sensitivity, and price elasticity or in-elasticity.

You'll also need to do some market research to be able to predict how your rivals will respond to this aggressive pricing plan. For instance, if your opponent lowers his pricing in response to your low price, this will result in a dead end since you would then drop your price again, prompting him to respond similarly, and so on, with no one coming out ahead.

It's true what was previously mentioned, but it's also true that your price approach for market penetration may serve as a barrier to entry for new rivals. Because there is a very significant danger that a new entrant will get a large market share, they may decide not to join the market after realizing that their margin will be small given your cheap pricing.

However, in order for you to succeed with this plan and become the lowest-cost supplier in the market, you will need to be ready to take advantage of the economies of scale that come with significant sales volume.

If your rival is using a market penetration approach and you already have a firm, you need to do the same in-depth analysis of the industry and your own capabilities:

- Is cutting expenses something you can really do?
- Is there a guarantee it will yield large quantities?
- Can you accept the chance of offering your product for a cheap price in the hopes that high volume sales will provide you with the desired market share and profitability?

If the answers to any of these questions are unfavorable, you should carefully analyze this penetration approach before implementing it. If you're still unsure, don't use the method.

But if you're a startup company owner thinking about using this tactic in a niche sector with little competition, concentrate on finding ways to cut expenses and increase productivity.

Whichever pricing method you choose, be sure to include it in your marketing mix plan along with the rationale behind your decision.

At the time of your business plan update, at least once a year, review your selected marketing approach, including your pricing strategy, to make sure it is the best one for your product in light of the market, your customers, and your competitors.

Promotional Pricing

When a new product is introduced, promotional pricing is often employed. It's used to boost demand for goods whose sales are trailing behind. Those who are seeking a bargain are often the price-target purchasers. Special events are intended for some of these promotional event price examples. These are often reserved for special occasions, such as Christmas or Easter.

While purchasing a house, there are allowances or rebate schemes available. On occasion, the seller will provide a move-in allowance, reimbursement for renovations, a move-in allowance, or a refund for all cash, eliminating the need for financing or large purchases like vehicles. Numerous retailers promote interest-free financing options for their furniture purchases.

These price plans are also available at car dealerships for models from prior years. These tactics have been quite effective in the sales sector, but you must take caution while using them since clients are starting to recognize the genuine worth of the tactics. Obtain two for the price of one or purchase one, get one free is another phase method that seems to be effective.

This is feasible in the event of an excessive inventory load, cheap product costs, and a strong profit margin. An additional significant payment option is an extended payment period.

Deposits and payments must be made gradually. Only when you have made a payment will you be able to get the product. This is a fairly typical practice in the building and restoration industries, where payments are received as soon as the job is started, halfway through, and finally when it is finished.

Occasionally, these company methods benefit from free or inexpensive warranties. A satisfied consumer seldom returns a quality product. Consequently, these tactics have a favorable effect. Customers are becoming skeptical as a result of the overuse of these tactics. They search for the deal's actuality. The "going out of business" deal is the most popular kind of promotional pricing.

This deal could mislead; therefore, it might be deceptive. This is a move for the same company. You should know as a consumer that you are not being tricked into any such plan. Make wise decisions while creating your price strategy since there are still plenty of successful promotional pricing schemes available.

Including a Discount in Your Pricing Strategy

Setting a price for products is hard. There isn't a single, all-encompassing magic formula that can determine the ideal pricing for a product. While there isn't a foolproof plan, there are steps that may be taken to improve pricing strategies. Since one can only depend on their own judgment when making price judgments, it is impossible to be certain. However, choices are never entirely satisfying, even when they are made.

One of the most important decisions in a company is determining the pricing of products or services. Products must be priced such that both the target market and the firm can benefit from them, or else the business will fail to make a profit in the long run.

Pricing may be approached from a variety of non-scientific and scientific angles. A pricing methodology that considers your expenses, the impact of competition, and the value perception of your customers is provided below.

Sometimes, pricing rules used in marketing go overlooked. They should be considered with the same care as marketing and advertising strategies since they may have a significant impact on earnings. Price variations have a significant impact on sales volume and gross margins. Through lower storage costs, for example, or by opening up options for bulk discounts with suppliers, this has indirect implications for other costs.

You may consider offering discounts to customers who provide you with a competitive edge while developing your pricing strategy.

Cash reductions might be given to clients who make their payments on time. Thus, this method incentivizes individuals who assist their organization in preserving a steady, positive cash flow and lowering credit collection expenses.

When the cost of selling or delivering a product decreases with increased quantity, it becomes financially advantageous to provide bulk discounts for large orders. For example, a caterer may complete an order for twelve cupcakes for a single client at a price of ten cents each, but cupcakes that are displayed in the bakery might be sold to several customers for twenty cents apiece throughout the course of the day.

This is done in order to account for the possibility that some of the cupcakes won't sell. Maintaining the shop open for the convenience of sporadic consumers comes with costs as well. The shop incurs expenses in order to remain open for the convenience of random consumers.

Customers that basically help a business balance its cash flow and satisfy production objectives are rewarded with seasonal discounts.

Trade-in allowances are advantageous to both businesses and customers when they are used for returned, used products that may be repurposed or sold profitably.

Economically speaking, promotional allowances often make sense. For example, your marketing efforts will have more clout if your product is included in advertisements or other promotional activities run by a retail chain that also sells it. Should this be the case, you may decide to provide the retail chain that does so with a price reduction.

Alternative pricing strategies

Undoubtedly, one of the most crucial elements of your marketing mix is pricing. The commercial success or failure of your product might be determined by its price. When promoting your goods, you need to consider the following factors:

It must be of the highest caliber.

It needs to have characteristics that your customers want or need.

It needs to be distinct from what your rivals are selling.

It ought to have a sensible budget.

Additionally, you have to focus on an effective marketing effort.

It's critical to choose a price plan that will enable you to effectively sell your goods in the market while keeping these considerations in mind.

Here are a few different pricing approaches:

1. Economic or generic pricing: In this tactic, the cheap price draws in the customer. That is characteristic of

budget or generic brands. You need to have a low-cost structure, basic functionality, and advertising for this method to work. Make sure you experience some strong, consistent results at the same time.

2. Differential pricing: This pricing strategy bases prices on a number of factors, including the type of buyer (e.g., prices for department stores, online stores, and retail stores differ); geographic location (prices in California may be higher than in Illinois); quantity purchased (buyers of large quantities will receive a different rate than those of small quantities); and national account segment (prices charged to a national account will differ from those charged to a local account). Remember that differential pricing cannot be used without good justification.

3. Premium pricing: This approach works well for high-end or luxury products like jewels, yachts, estates, and aircraft.

If the market perceives your product as a high-end or luxury good, you may use this tactic.

4. Pricing for captive products or companion products: This tactic may also be used for product line pricing. In this instance, the goods are priced and packaged as companions. (a bowl and mixer, for example). Additionally, they see some items as prisoners (such as a razor that requires a certain kind of blade to operate). Frequently, these goods come in a single bundle. (For instance, the razor may come with blades.) When these goods are purchased without a bundle, their costs are often greater.

Prior to selecting a certain approach, don't forget to thoroughly examine your items to ensure that the cost is reasonable.

How Do You Know If Your Pricing Is Right?

Even if you have the best product or service in the world, you won't succeed if your pricing is off. Three main pricing systems are used by internet businesses: VAPS, CAPS, and POPS. When done correctly, they can only assist businesses in getting an edge over their competitors.

Selling a tangible product that is distributed to your consumers is a successful way to implement the tangible objective pricing strategy (POPS). Wall-Mart and Amazon.com belong to this group. These companies begin by calculating the cost of producing and delivering one more product in order to establish the starting price. The marginal cost is what it is.

Let's use Walmart as an example. They market microwaves. How much would it cost them to sell one more unit? They would need to ascertain the costs associated with purchasing from their suppliers, placing it in the shop, and carrying out the transaction in order to come up with this amount. Therefore, a corporation must increase the marginal cost in order to establish the ultimate price.

The operational profit margin is as follows:

They must compare it with comparable businesses in order to determine the percentage. Amazon made a profit of 6%. Rival stores have to strive for the same operating margin, while a smaller one would suffice. By creating an effective business process, a company may reduce expenses and maintain a competitive edge while maintaining low costs.

Price Strategy for Acquisition at a Cost (CAPS) POPS works well if the cost of the real goods you are providing is your main expense. However, companies that offer goods or services where the ultimate pricing is determined by marketing and the volume of visits to their website may find it advantageous to use CAPS. CAPS often provides answers to two main queries.

1. How much will it cost to attract visitors to a website?
2. What proportion of site visitors would really make a purchase?

To get the company's cost per acquisition, divide the response to the first question by the response to the second. As a result, the ultimate price may be calculated by adding the operational profit margin to this.

For instance, a store may discover that, on average, a visitor to the website spends $0.10 and that, on average, 1% of visitors complete a transaction. We then just need to calculate the cost per acquisition from here. And we ascertain the appropriate ultimate cost. Reducing the cost per acquisition is crucial in this situation.

The strategy of value-added pricing, or VAPS, is for companies selling digital goods like e-books and online courses, where the marginal cost is $0. VAPS functions best when you have a business plan that allows you to bill various customers at various rates.

www.ingramcontent.com/pod-product-compliance
Lightning Source LLC
Chambersburg PA
CBHW072209290526
45794CB00004B/1698